AARON BROOKS

RISE
ABOVE

Positively for Kids®
Kirkland Avenue Office Park
8II Kirkland Avenue, Suite 200
Kirkland, WA 98033
www.positivelyforkids.com

Brooks, Aaron, 1976-

Aaron Brooks—Rise Above / by Aaron Brooks with Greg Brown.

48 p.: ill. (mostly col.), ports.; 26 cm. (Positively For Kids)

Summary: Aaron Brooks tells how he used his positive vision, goal-setting, and hard work
to rise from humble beginnings to a successful career as a starting quarterback in the NFL.
Audience: Grades 4-8

ISBN 0-9634650-9-0

I. Brooks, Aaron, 1976- .Juvenile literature. 2. Football players—United States—
Biography—Juvenile literature. [I. Brooks, Aaron, 1976 –.2. Football players—Biography.]
I. Brown, Greg, 1957- . II. Title.

796.332/092—dc2I [B]

Library of Congress Control Number:
2004III253

Photo Credits:
All photos courtesy of Aaron Brooks and family except the following:
Brian Alston: 3I bottom right; 47 left. AP/Wide World: 30 middle; 32; 34 right; 36;
37; 39 top left; 39 bottom right; 40 top right; 40 bottom right; 42 middle. Dan Bruton:
4I top left. Rich Chamless: I5 left; I5 right; I6 bottom right; 43 bottom left. Tom Dipace:
6; 35; 39 bottom left; 39 middle left; 40 left; 4I top right; 46. Pete Emerson: 28 left.
Ferguson High School Annual: 25 left; 25 right. Getty Images: cover; 27; 29; 34 left;
39 top right; 4I bottom; 42 top; 45. Dan Grogan: 28 left. James Johnson: 47 middle.
Bill Vaughan Jr.: 42 bottom. Copyright © I997, Vicki Cronis/*The Virginian-Pilot* reprinted
with permission: 30 left. Joan Wilt: 22; 47 right.

Special Thanks:
Positively For Kids would like to thank the people and organizations that helped make
this book possible: Aaron and Tisa Brooks; their families and friends; Dan Bruton of
Marketing I0I; and the New Orleans Saints.

Book Design:
Methodologie, Inc., Seattle

Printed in Canada

AARON BROOKS

RISE
ABOVE

BY **AARON BROOKS**
WITH **GREG BROWN**

A POSITIVELY FOR KIDS BOOK

Hey y'all. What's up?

I'm Aaron Brooks, and I'm a starting quarterback
in the National Football League.

There are only 32 openings in the world for the
job I do. That's how many teams there are in the
NFL. So, I guess you can say just playing quarterback in the NFL means I've made it to the top of
my sport.

I've been blessed with a perfect quarterback
body—6-foot-4, 215 pounds, with foot speed and
a cannon arm. I had the framework, but to get
where I am, I needed a game plan and the strength
to follow it. For me to rise above took the same
steps it takes for anyone to be successful in life.

I've been on winning teams and some losing
teams. I've set records at every level. I've led amazing comebacks and thrown untimely interceptions.
I know the elation of helping the New Orleans
Saints to their first playoff win in team history.
And I know the frustration of being overshadowed
and overlooked. Eight quarterbacks were drafted
ahead of me.

YEAR 2003

YEAR 1986

To get to the top, I've scratched my way up from "The Bottom."

That's what folks call the part of town where I came up—The Bottom. It's a place like many in America, where hope for a better life is blocked by a culture of negativity. Where generations waste their days and their lives on street corners. A place where single moms need government assistance to feed and clothe their children.

I know it well. I spent my first 18 years at the bottom. I lived in the public projects, survived on food stamps and free school lunches. I know the anger that embeds in you from being poor in the richest country. I know the ache of longing for my father's love and attention.

Back in the day I made myself a promise—a promise to rise above the bottom.

I've written this book to help young readers who need some hope and direction. I'm here to say you can "Rise Above!"

> These are believed to be the two earliest pictures of me. You can see my bowed legs as Pop gets down to our level with Duke on his knee.

> Duke and I in the tub with our toys.

My rise started on March 24, 1976, in the old brick Whittaker Hospital. The building is still there but the hospital was boarded up in the 1990s. I was born to Catherine Brooks, her third and final child. The story goes that I was supposed to be named Antwain. But nobody at the hospital knew how to spell it on the birth certificate so it was shortened to Aaron. For the longest time, I thought my middle name was Lynnette. I found out in elementary school that it's Lafette.

Newport News, Virginia, is where I grew up. It's a port city along the state's southern coast named after the News brothers or the "news" that ship captains brought to the early colonies. Nobody is sure which.

Like many from my area, my parents never married. My father, Fred Jones, worked as a longshoreman unloading ship cargo. We call him Pop.

I have a sister, Terrell, and a brother, Darren. We call him Duke. Terrell is seven years older, and has a daughter named Jalyn. Duke is three years older, and has a son named Kamren.

Mom raised us the best she could. She worked different jobs and thankfully accepted public housing, government cheese, and food stamps to help us make it. She worked at the Crab Factory for a time. Even for those at the bottom, you didn't want anyone to know your momma worked at the Crab Factory. That was really scraping the barrel. She did what she had to do.

We lived in two different row apartments in the government's Section 8 housing projects. We were kicked out of the projects when I was in high school because Duke got in some trouble with the law. When that happens, the whole family is punished and we were evicted. Luckily we found a low-, low-rent apartment 20 blocks uptown to avoid homelessness.

As a young kid, I didn't know how poor we were. I didn't realize the sacrifices Mom made for us. Mom was loving, but real strict. She wasn't going to take any kid disrespecting her. She had two main rules: respect her and elders and be inside before dark. Mom had a heavy hand when it came to discipline. I learned quickly to say "Yes, sir" and "Yes, ma'am" to adults. As I got older, she was all up in my business. We always had to leave notes whenever we left the house. We never knew when Mom might show up to check on us.

I'm told I was an easy-going child. When I was a toddler, my legs worried Mom. They were so bowed, Mom said "you could drive a car through them." She got advice to massage my legs three times a day to help straighten the curves. It seemed to work.

When Mom called us in, or when she told us to stay inside if she left to run errands, I minded her. Mom knew that nothing good happened around our neighborhood at night. Indoors we passed a lot of time playing video games. Back in my day, we had old-school games, like Atari Asteroids® and boxing. We had this rickety old TV that needed coat-hangers for the antenna and pliers to change the channel. Mom always worried our video games would knock out her TV.

"YOU'D BETTER NOT WRECK THAT TV WITH THOSE VIDEO GAMES, YOU HEAR ME!" SHE SAID.

Newport News, VA

Pop was around for us when we were young. He visited and took us to fun places—to high school and college games and the circus. As I got older and walked around a lot, I'd walk by the Longshoremen's Union building on the way to the Boys & Girls Club and give him a holler. If we needed some money, Pop would give us what he had.

My world consisted of a 15-block area. Everything was within walking distance.

I don't remember ever going hungry. We had many hotdog and hamburger dinners and lots of cereal. Mom bought 13 boxes of cereal every grocery trip. I do remember the steamy summer nights trying to sleep without air conditioning. I shared a room with Duke. If you weren't next to the window to catch a breeze on those hot, sticky, humid East Coast nights, you had to sweat it out. I started in a bunk bed on top until I fell out.

I suffered a few injuries in my youth. A car hit me as I crossed a street when I was 7. My shirt got caught on the license plate as I fell down under the car between the tires, and the car dragged me about 20 feet. I walked away with minor scrapes on my arms and legs.

Another time I cut my big toe real bad on a piece of glass in a pool we called "Deadman's Pool." A few people had died in the outdoor pool—at least that's what we heard.

I almost choked to death (not really, it just seemed like it) when I ate some bony fish and a bone stuck in my throat. I didn't eat fish for a long time, but I like seafood now.

My worst cut came from teasing a girl when I was about 9 years old. We were walking down the street and I made fun of this girl. Actually, I was laughing at a picture of her. She didn't appreciate it and started at me. I turned to get away and ran smack into a telephone pole. Bamm! I hit headfirst and split my forehead wide open.

I didn't cry at first. Then my forehead gushed blood. That scared me. I needed four stitches at the hospital. You can't even see the scar anymore.

MY SCARS ARE ALL ON THE INSIDE. WHEN THERE IS SO MUCH NEGATIVITY AROUND, IT'S HARD NOT TO BE SUCKED DOWN BY IT. YOU GET THIS HOSTILITY THAT BURNS INSIDE. IF YOU LET IT, THE ANGER EATS UP YOUR SPIRIT.

So many kids from the bottom grow up with this "I don't give a ____" attitude. You could see it when I was coming up. I saw it in some of my friends.

First there's boredom. When kids are just hanging around with nothing to do, unsupervised day after day, it always leads to trouble. Then there's the loss of hope and ambition. Generation after generation of failure makes you believe nothin' is ever going to change, so why bother.

In the land of opportunity, there are teenagers who accept that. They're like, "So long, future, whatever." They have no goals. So they look for shortcuts to happiness. They turn to the streets.

And the streets offer nothing but dead ends. The fast life has many lanes—drugs, gaming (scamming others or stealing), prostitution, and other illegal activities. All those roads lead to addiction, jail, or death.

Kids grow up without values or principles. They drop out of school without any skills. A young girl gets pregnant and the whole cycle starts over again.

Mom always preached the importance of family, values of life, and education.

I had some close friends who went the wrong direction. And I almost did, too.

I'm not going to lie to you and say I was a perfect little angel growing up. I accidentally almost burned down our apartment when I was 9.

EVERYONE WAS DOWNSTAIRS. I WAS UPSTAIRS IN THE BATHROOM. I STARTED PLAYING WITH A BOOK OF MATCHES. I HEARD SOMEBODY COMING, SO I SHOOK THE MATCH TO PUT IT OUT AND THREW IT BEHIND THE TOILET. I THOUGHT IT WENT OUT. ABOUT 5 MINUTES LATER WE HAD A BIG OL' FIRE IN THE BATHROOM.

I ran back into bed and got under the covers. I pretended to be asleep. Mom smelled the smoke and ran upstairs.

"What the hell happened?" she screamed.

"I don't know," I lied. "I didn't do it."

Thankfully, Mom put out the fire. To this day, I don't like my wife burning candles at home. It makes me nervous. Saints coach Mike McCarthy leaves candles burning all night. I tell him he's going to burn down the facility some day.

I'm not proud to admit I got into a few fights and stole some things as a young teen.

The fights were self-defense. For example, I was walking down the street on my way home from elementary school when I saw a group of guys trying to sneak up and jump me. I could always run well. I just outran them. A few days later I saw one of them alone and I punched him.

Duke and my older cousins were well known in the "'hood." Duke protected me through his reputation. Everyone knew if they messed with me they would mess with Duke. So I really didn't have many people breathing down my neck.

The hardest thing when you're young is to say no to your friends. I didn't at first. They'd say, "Aaron, let's go mess around," and we did.

I went along and stole a few things before I reached high school. The first thing I stole was clothes. I took them straight off clotheslines in our neighborhood. I tried stealing a few other little things, Now & Laters®, cookies, and ice cream bars, but I wasn't very successful. I was caught red-handed once and let go. I've never been arrested.

When you are busted, it makes you think if what you are doing is worth it. You hear of kids getting shot trying to take this and that. I knew I wasn't willing to die for any amount of money or anything. About that time I turned away from the streets, thanks to sports, my family, the Boys Club, my coaches, mentors who were people of character, and the local library.

Duke and my cousins, Greg and Ricky, were big sports guys. We had this overflowing box of sports equipment at home—bats, baseballs, tennis balls, footballs, basketballs, football pads, mitts, everything. I was the youngest of the four and they dragged me along.

We played all sorts of made-up sports in the grassy field between the row apartments or in the streets.

> **My hangouts: The Dunbar field where I played all kinds of sports; the Pearl Bailey Library, my favorite study spot in high school; my first home at Harbor Homes; the Boys & Girls Club, which gave me a place to play; my second home at Ridley Circle, where everyone dried their clothes on lines.**

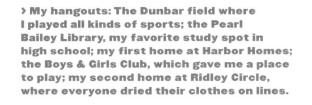

> I deliver a fastball during a Little League game.

> Terrell, Duke, and I smile for the camera.

Aaron Brooks
The Newport News boy, 12, pitched a 1-hitter and scored twice to lead the Anderson Park Little League All-Stars to an 8-1 win over the Williams-burg All-Stars for the Williamsburg Moose Invitational title.

> This old pier at Lincoln Park is where I used to spend hours catching crabs with chicken backs and nets. Storms wrecked the pier and it's never been repaired.

We played baseball with a tennis ball and teams of four—a pitcher, a catcher, and two outfielders. We played basketball. And we played forms of football.

Before I was big enough, I used to be the designated pass rusher. Then they put me in suicide football gear—those cheap plastic helmets and foam pads. The older guys would wear the real stuff. They'd throw me the ball and say, "Run the ball, boy." Then they'd tackle me real hard and make me run again and again.

We used to play little games around the way. One game we called "Hotball." It was like rugby with four to 10 players. You started with a football on the ground. Everyone would try to tackle whoever picked up the ball. If you were tackled, you had to throw the ball in the air. The object was to try and outrun everyone and score a touchdown. I got pretty good at eluding tacklers—it proved to be good scrambling practice.

We also played "sidewalk football." If we were walking to the Boys Club or to football practice we'd play a game on the sidewalk. We'd use a sock, pad, piece of paper, or T-shirt as a football. One guy would be behind and we'd throw him the "ball." Then he'd try to break through tackles while staying on the narrow side-walk. The grass was out of bounds, too. We didn't really tackle each other on the concrete, we just tried to grab and stop each other. If you broke through the group it was a touchdown. That person would then break into an imitation of our favorite running back at the time, such as Eric Dickerson, Tony Dorsett, or Walter Payton.

I FIRST DISCOVERED I HAD A GOOD ARM BY PLAYING LITTLE LEAGUE BASEBALL.

We had a nice little ball field down by the waterfront. It doesn't look so nice now and the league is down from about 10 teams in my day to about four teams.

I was a good pitcher and threw hard. I had a couple one-hitters. I also played shortstop. You can see from my baseball pictures why my family used to call me "Legs." I could hit well. I wasn't a Barry Bonds, but I hit for average and was on base all the time. I was fast enough that I could hit in-the-park home runs if my hit went between the outfielders.

My greatest Little League game came during an All-Star tournament in Williamsburg. I hit three home runs in one game and finished with four during the weekend competition. Another guy had five home runs and beat me out for the tournament Most Valuable Player award.

In third grade people took notice of my throwing ability when I won the softball throw contest at our Hidenwood Elementary Field Day. I *launched* it. The adults were like, "Wow!" They were amazed how far it went and everyone said what a strong arm I had.

For some time I thought basketball was my game. I played AAU hoops for Boo Williams. We went to a lot of summer basketball tournaments; most we traveled to by car. I experienced my first plane ride at 10 when our basketball team went to the nationals in Kansas.

› Standing tall ready to hit.

› Mom and her boys proudly display some hardware.

WE HAD TO RAISE ABOUT $300 EACH FOR THE EXPENSES. I HATED GOING DOOR TO DOOR ASKING FOR DONATIONS. **I LOVED THE TRIP, THOUGH.**

We finished 28th out of 48 teams. One of my AAU teammates was future NBA star Allen Iverson.

The first year I was old enough to play tackle football I told Pop I didn't want to play. I changed my mind the next year when I was 8 years old. I started at running back. I wasn't any bigger than anyone else. I didn't hit my growth spurt until eighth grade. Although I loved everyone at the Boys Club, where I spent hours after school, I played football for their rival, a youth club called Doris Miller. We had talented teams. All my years in youth football, I'd say we lost only two games. I played youth football through seventh grade.

› My favorite Mariner receiver Eric Jones.

At the start of eighth grade my friends told me the high school junior varsity coach wanted me to turn out for his team. Ferguson High included grades 9-12, but top middle-school athletes were allowed to play for the high school team.

"Naah. You guys are joking me," I said to my friends.

"FOR REAL! FOR REAL, MAN," THEY SAID. "HE WANTS YOU TO PLAY."

So I turned out for the school team instead of playing my last year in youth football. Once I got out there Coach Bynum saw I had a good arm. He told me I could be the quarterback.

When you start playing high school sports, things can get serious, especially in football and basketball. It was tough being a skinny little eighth grader playing with 16- and 17-year-olds. After a few weeks of practice I started to realize I could do it. I could compete.

Unfortunately, our team didn't compete well. We lost all eight of our JV games. It's one of the most embarrassing seasons I've seen. We did some good things and I played well at times.

Next year, when I was a ninth grader, the head football coach, Steve Isley, called me up to play on varsity by the end of the season. I played all three sports that year for the Ferguson Mariners—football, basketball, and baseball.

A turning point came for me in ninth grade. I thought I was the man.

Things came pretty easy for me in school but I wasn't doing the work. I was getting a lot of Ds on my report card. By the end of the year I woke up to the fact I had to buckle down.

A passionate new head football coach, Tommy Reamon, took over my sophomore year. Reamon, a former NFL player, put a lot of faith in me to be a team leader. He took me to a top-rated summer football camp, at his own expense, and helped me envision what I could become—a big-time college quarterback.

With that goal, we laid out a step-by-step plan of how I could get there. The plan took focus both on the physical side, building my body and skills, and the mental side, improving my study skills and grades.

I started spending time at the Pearl Bailey Public Library. For real, for real. I walked by it all the time. So I'd stop in after practice and spend some time studying and reading. It was quiet. When I was finished with my homework, I'd read for pleasure, maybe about sports stars or whatever caught my eye that day.

I had to fight extra hard to get my grade-point average back up after my slow start. And every summer I went to summer school. But I finished with a 2.5 grade-point average and passed my college entrance exam on my first try, thanks to a tutor. Throughout my last three years of high school, my mom, my school guidance counselor Tom McGrann, assistant principal Joan Wilt, and Coach Reamon helped me stay on top of my grades.

> My teammate Antwain Smith, who also scored more than 1,000 points in his high school basketball career.

MY JUNIOR YEAR I CAME INTO MY OWN. ONE RAINY NIGHT, WITH ABOUT 15 PEOPLE IN THE STANDS, AN NFL SCOUT TOLD JAMES "POO" JOHNSON, A MENTOR FROM THE BOYS CLUB, THAT I COULD THROW ACROSS THE FIELD AS WELL AS ANY PROFESSIONAL QUARTERBACK.

That year I threw a pass to our all-state receiver Eric Jones during practice. He came back to the huddle with his right hand bleeding. My bullet pass cut a hole between his pinkie and ring fingers.

By my senior year I was on fire on the football field. I finished my high school career passing for 4,396 yards and 42 touchdowns.

None of my high school football teams had winning records, though. I think those losing years prepared me for college and the pros. It toughened me up mentally. I never lost my confidence despite the losses. I always believed I could do the job. Once you believe you're a loser, then you are.

One memorable showdown football game happened my senior year against rival Bethel. Some don't know this, but Allen Iverson was a heck of a high school quarterback. He was the better runner; I was the better passer. We squared off and Bethel had the better team.

After being down 15-7 in the first half, we fought back. The fourth quarter our teams combined for a wild 56 points. We lost 56-29. Iverson ran for 165 yards and three touchdowns (throwing for another score). I passed for a career-high 284 yards and three TDs. I ran in another score.

FUN FACT >>> THE FERGUSON FOOTBALL TEAMS WERE 5-5 AARON'S FRESHMAN YEAR, 1-10 HIS SOPHOMORE YEAR, AND 3-7 BOTH HIS JUNIOR AND SENIOR YEARS.

23

> Eric, Antwain, and me on high school graduation day.

THE GAME EVERYONE REMEMBERS, HOWEVER, IS THE 1993 DISTRICT BASKETBALL GAME BETWEEN BETHEL AND FERGUSON. ALLEN AND I WENT AT IT WITH A TRIP TO THE STATE TOURNAMENT ON THE LINE. THE NEWSPAPER CALLED THE GAME "A MASTERPIECE."

We were trading baskets all game long. We led by 10 most of the game. Allen staged heroics down the stretch by knocking down 3s from NBA range and finished with 41 points. I scored 19 and had a chance to win it at the end with a drive down the lane. My foot slipped and I missed the shot. Bethel won 81-78 and went on to claim the state title that year.

Our basketball teams were very successful my last two years at Ferguson. We went 16-8 and 20-5. I scored 1,069 high school points.

Choosing a college was a critical decision. I had a lot of options. That's what high school and college are all about, so you have options. I received scholarship offers from colleges all over the country, but it came down to two schools—Maryland and the University of Virginia.

I wanted to stay close to home and I wanted to play quarterback. My assistant principal, Mrs. Wilt, who is a big Cavaliers fan, suggested I look at the U of Va. I took a recruiting trip and was impressed. I did some homework on both schools and found Maryland had never played a black quarterback. Virginia had. I became a Virginia Cavalier.

AARON BROOKS HIGH SCHOOL ACHIEVEMENTS

- Voted "Best All-Around" and "Most Athletic" by his high school peers
- Earned All-Peninsula District football honors junior and senior years
- Voted Most Valuable Player by football teammates his last two years
- Earned All-District Basketball first team senior year
- Nominated for McDonald's High School All-American Basketball Team
- Basketball team captain and MVP as a senior
- Lettered three years in football, four years in basketball, twice in baseball

Attending college proved to be a great experience for me. Not only did it make me a well-rounded person, it helped me see beyond "The Bottom." I met, worked with, and dealt with all sorts of people. It's also where I met my wife.

The Virginia freshman football class of 1994 became life-long friends of mine. We had a group of about 10 who stayed in the program and stayed together. They all are quality guys. Many came from quality families, too. Hanging around them my freshman year opened my eyes.

I saw the dads of my friends around at practices and games. They supported their sons and were there for them. I saw what I was missing: my father's love and attention.

MY DAD SORT OF CHECKED OUT OF MY LIFE WHEN I REACHED MY LATE TEEN YEARS. I GUESS HE FIGURED I WAS AN ADULT AND DIDN'T NEED HIM ANYMORE. BUT I NEEDED HIM JUST AS MUCH THEN. A DAD SHOULD STICK AROUND FOR LIFE.

So this pain built up every time I saw the other dads. I finally had to do something about it. So I wrote my dad a hate letter. With my tears dropping on the paper, I told him how much it hurt me that he didn't seem interested in me anymore. I asked him, "Why aren't you around? Why can't you come and see me? Why can't you come check me out playing football?"

I didn't write it to make Pop feel guilty. I wanted him to know I needed him. It was the only way I could rise above my pain. I had to let out those feelings. For me that was enough. I said what I had to say.

My mother gave Pop the letter and to this day he has never said anything to me about it. But he did make some changes. He got back together with Mom, for starters. And he has come back into my life and been to many of my college and pro games.

The only way to see me play my first two years of college was to watch practices. My first year I red-shirted, meaning I could practice but couldn't play in games. Many freshman are held back a year from playing so they can mature. I knew it was in the plan so I was patient. The next season I stood on the sidelines, waiting my turn.

FUN FACT >>> AARON SET A UNIVERSITY OF VIRGINIA SCHOOL RECORD WITH SIX CAREER 300-YARD PASSING GAMES.

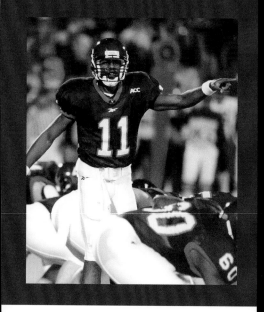

My sophomore season I split time with a fifth-year senior named Tim Sherman, the son of an assistant coach on the team. Head coach George Welsh would bring me in when the team was in trouble and needed a big play. The pressure situations combined with my inexperience led to some poor decisions on my part. I threw seven interceptions and one touchdown that year. I did show flashes of what I could do. We finished 7-5 thanks to the leadership of future NFL stars Tiki and Ronde Barber.

GETTING THAT TASTE OF BIG-TIME COLLEGE FOOTBALL, WITH 50,000 FANS AND TV AUDIENCES WATCHING, MADE ME WORK EVEN HARDER.

FUN FACT >>> AARON BECAME THE FIRST CAVALIERS QUARTERBACK IN 30 YEARS TO START EVERY CONTEST IN TWO STRAIGHT SEASONS.

My junior year I entered the 1997 season as the starting quarterback. We lost 16 starters so nobody knew what to expect from our inexperienced team. A rough start turned some Virginia fans against me. They talked trash about me in the newspapers and on the sports radio shows. They even booed me in our home stadium a few times.

It stung, no doubt about it. I think all athletes hope their fans stick with them through the ups and downs. But it showed me that the higher you get in sports, the less loyalty there is. It's all about results. Can you do the job? That's what counts. If you can't, coaches find someone else. I accept that deal. What upsets me is when our team, my teammates, or I don't get the respect earned.

After our slow start, we finished strong, winning six of our last eight games. We ended the season a respectable 7-4 by beating rival Virginia Tech 34-20. I set a school record with 390 passing yards. In our final month I had 14 touchdown passes. I was the hottest Atlantic Coast Conference quarterback the last month.

When the preseason picks came out for my senior season, "experts" rated two or three quarterbacks ahead of me. I used it as motivation.

FUN FACT >>> AARON LEFT VIRGINIA RANKED SECOND IN CAREER TD PASSES WITH 33 AND WAS THIRD ALL-TIME IN PASSING YARDS (5,118), ATTEMPTS (651), COMPLETIONS (357) AND TOTAL OFFENSE (5,665 YARDS)

29

We started the 1998 season doing our thing. We opened 5-0 and were ranked as high as fourth in the country. We had a bomb defense led by safety Anthony Poindexter, who could've been an NFL draft pick after his junior year but decided to come back for a national title run.

Our championship dreams were tripped up by a wild 41-38 loss to Georgia Tech and a 45-14 blowout defeat from Florida State. Anthony blew out his knee in the seventh game, and that knocked the wind out of us for awhile. Sports—and life—can deal some unfair, nasty blows, and this was one of them. We all were so torn up by his injury. It hit me hard because Anthony and I roomed together. Anthony recovered and played in the NFL with Cleveland and Baltimore. He returned to U.Va. to be the running backs coach.

Our final regular-season game against Virginia Tech looked bleak at half-time. We were down 29-7. To never give up is the true mark of someone who rises above. We rallied in the second half and outscored Tech 29-3. The last score came on a 93-yard drive and a 47-yard touchdown to Ahmad Hawkins with 2:01 to play for the thrilling 36-32 win.

IT MARKED THE BIGGEST COMEBACK IN CAVALIER HISTORY.

That helped us play in the Peach Bowl, where we faced Georgia. I wanted to win that game, my last in college, so much. But it wasn't meant to be. We blew a 21-0 lead and I threw an interception in the end zone with 4 minutes to go. I did bring us back with a 30-yard TD run with 90 seconds to play. We had a chance

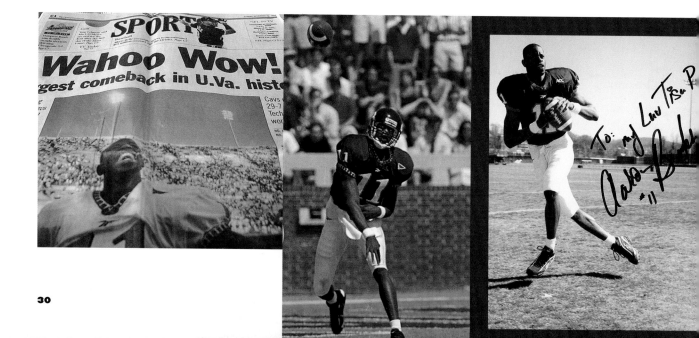

> My class teammates at the U of Va.: (front, left to right) Robert Hunt, Maurice Anderson, Anthony Poindexter, Wali Rainer; (back, left to right) Germane Crowell, Terrence Wilkins, me, and Jami'h Rainer.

> My wife Tisa.

> Graduation day.

at a game-winning field goal at the end but missed and lost 35-33. At the time, it felt like a dagger to my heart. We were so close to being the best team the University of Virginia had ever seen.

Looking back, my time at the University of Virginia was priceless. I earned my degree in anthropology, and during summer school after my second year I met Tisa Parker. She's a year older and wanted to be a teacher.

She saw my highs and lows on the field and I shared her personal family battle. My fifth year, her father, Dudley Parker Jr., found out he had cancer. I'd drive the hour trip with Tisa whenever she needed to go home. I went to the hospital many times to support the family. Eventually, I stood by Tisa at the funeral. I held her hand and gave her my support the whole way through. Real men don't run, they step up and stay close when times are tough. I guess I proved to her I would be around for the long run. We were married in June 2003.

HOW TO RISE ABOVE

- Have a vision of what you want to do
- Believe in that vision and commit to it
- Talk with professional people who have been there for guidance
- Find out requirements of how to get there
- Create a checklist of short- and long-term goals

- Get instruction on the skills you need
- Accept help from others
- Overcome setbacks
- Show your determination
- Do the work necessary

After my senior season I looked around the country at the top quarterbacks and compared my numbers to everyone else. I felt I belonged among the top names, so I felt good about the NFL draft.

Only the Pittsburgh Steelers gave me an official workout before the draft. Green Bay's quarterback coach, Mike McCarthy, dropped in and watched me throw. That was going to be it, but a snowstorm delayed his flight and gave us more time together. We went to the Virginia film room, where I broke down some of our game film and showed him I was a student of the game. I won Coach McCarthy over with that extra time.

Draft day was very disappointing. Round after round slipped by without my name being called. Eight other quarterbacks were selected ahead of me. Green Bay, at the urging of Coach McCarthy, picked me in the fourth round.

DESPITE MY INITIAL LETDOWN OF BEING OVERLOOKED, BEING WITH GREEN BAY PROVED TO BE A GREAT EXPERIENCE. TO RISE ABOVE, YOU HAVE TO TURN PERCEIVED SETBACKS INTO POSITIVES.

Even though I didn't play a single down in a game my rookie season, I got a quarterback education by watching Brett Favre up close.

I saw him engineer a fantastic home comeback. He'd come off the field gasping for air, asking "Where's the oxygen tank?" and then a few minutes later go out and make spectacular plays. His will to win is amazing.

Plus, I was able to pick his brain. One day I asked him what he considered his best game. He said it was a game against the Chicago Bears. That day I went to our video guy and asked him to make me a copy of that game. I took it home and watched it over and over.

When you're a rookie, asking for pointers and learning how other people do your job is a key to rising in any business.

FUN FACT >>> AARON WAS THE TOP-RATED QB IN THE 2000 POSTSEASON (92.0 RATING), COMPLETING 46 OF 77 PASSES FOR 561 YARDS AND SIX TDS.

33

> Brett Favre and I congratulate each other after a game.

The Packers decided to make some changes at the top after the 1999 season, and it trickled down to me. Coach Ray Rhodes and some of his staff were fired. Coach McCarthy landed in New Orleans with the Saints as their new offensive coordinator. He wanted me. So the Saints worked out a deal that sent me south to be the backup to starter Jeff Blake.

The Saints got off to a fantastic 6-0 start in 2000. Then fate threw a twist. Blake hurt his ankle against the Oakland Raiders in week 11. I went into the huddle and said, "OK, I'm next."

My first NFL pass was picked off by Raiders cornerback Charles Woodson. My second pass, though, was a 53-yard TD bomb to Willie Jackson.

I'VE NEVER HAD A PROBLEM WITH CONFIDENCE. SOME SAY I'M OVERCONFIDENT. STILL, OTHERS THOUGHT I ACTED TOO CALM. I NEVER UNDERSTOOD THAT. DON'T YOU WANT YOUR QUARTERBACK TO BE UNDER CONTROL? THEY WORRIED WHETHER I COULD BE A LEADER.

FUN FACT >>> AARON BECAME THE FIRST NFL QB TO HAVE A 400-YARD PASSING EFFORT AND A 100-YARD RUSHING GAME IN THE SAME SEASON AND ONLY THE SIXTH PLAYER TO HAVE BOTH IN A CAREER.

When Blake went down, I knew this was my chance. I had a solid outing with 187 yards passing and two touchdown passes.

The next week I made my first NFL start—against the defending Super Bowl champs St. Louis Rams. I ran for two touchdowns and passed for another to become only the third quarterback to beat a defending Super Bowl champion in his first start.

The following week I set a team record with 441 passing yards. Later that season I ran for 108 yards in a game to set a Saints rushing record for a quarterback.

The highlight of the 2000 season came after we qualified for the playoffs with a 10-6 record. Those who aren't Saints fans have to understand that in the 36-year history of the team, the Saints have had only eight winning seasons. Before 2000, New Orleans had been in the playoffs only four times and had never won a playoff game—ever!

The history of losing didn't bother me. I didn't have anything to do with that, so I didn't feel jinxed. Each season is a new chance. The past is the past.

We matched up against the Rams in the NFL Wild Card game. We put together a great plan and team effort and made history with a 31-24 victory. Our owner, Tom Benson, danced on the field with joy. It was crazy. It was unbelievable. It was fun to see the fans enjoying the moment.

It almost didn't matter to Saints fans that we lost in the next round to Minnesota. It mattered to us players. I was put to the test and came in to get it done. The coaches gave me an ultimatum to win or go home.

I can honestly say the most nervous I've ever been wasn't during the playoffs. It hit that spring.

My high school in Newport News was shut down a few years after I left. The district built two new schools, one called Heritage High. They invited me back that spring of 2001 to present their state-winning basketball team with championship rings.

I didn't have much public speaking experience. I was knee-shaking nervous and it showed.

Going into the 2001 season I was a little edgy for a different reason. I thought I had proved myself. The Saints kept me in the dark as to who would be the starting quarterback, Blake or myself. It was stressful. I didn't want to share my starting position.

The media wanted Jeff and I to turn on each other but we never did. We kept our comments professional and respectful toward each other.

EXPECTATIONS WERE HIGH. IN TRAINING CAMP, I GOT THE NOD TO BE THE NO. 1 QUARTERBACK AND STARTED ALL 16 GAMES.

A scary thing happened in early November. In a loss to the New York Jets, a safety tackled me by my facemask, twisting me to the ground and almost ripping off my helmet.

Late in the season we were on pace to make the playoffs again at 7-5. But we lost our last four games. I think some guys packed it in. It's part of the same old story of people letting history drag them down. It's a hard cycle to break. To me, quitting when you still have a chance is unacceptable.

The 2002 season began on an upswing. I signed a contract extension with the team and we won our first three games. Unfortunately we lost our last three of five games, to finish 9-7 and just miss the playoffs. Those last three losses were by a total of 12 points. While it was frustrating, everyone fought hard until the end. You can live with that. The bounces just didn't go our way. In our loss to Minnesota, Daunte Culpepper fumbled the shotgun snap, kicked the ball, then picked it up for the game-winning touchdown run.

FUN FACT >>> AARON WAS 16 FOR 29 FOR 266 YARDS AND FOUR TOUCHDOWN PASSES IN THE SAINTS PLAYOFF WIN.

I underwent my first major surgery after the 2002 season. My shoulder bothered me late in the season. Doctors determined the seriousness after the season. I didn't feel sorry for myself for one second or ask, "Why me?"

I found out what needed to be done to fix the problem. So I had surgery just after the season ended. I focused hard on what I needed to do each day to get my throwing motion back. I started throwing again in May and was ready to go by the start of camp. When I have a challenge, I'm very good at focusing my efforts. I visualize the outcome and concentrate on what needs to be done.

The 2003 season again proved how small the difference is between NFL playoff teams and those who stay home. We were 8-8, but three losses were so close, one an overtime defeat. We did finish stronger by winning our last game.

The most interesting play of the season happened at Jacksonville in December. A desperation final play covered 75 yards for a score after the football was touched by five players. I threw it to Donté Stallworth, who pitched it to Michael Lewis, who flipped it to Deuce McAllister, who tossed it across the field to Jerome Pathon. I made the final block to help Pathon score.

> The Saints made a TV commercial where we "replayed" the River City Relay in a grocery store with a loaf of bread.

> Those who had a hand in the River City Relay: (left to right) me, Stallworth, Lewis, Pathon, and McAllister.

THE PLAY, CALLED **THE RIVER CITY RELAY,** WAS HONORED AT THE 2004 ESPY AWARDS AS THE PLAY OF THE YEAR. **THE NFL ALSO NAMED IT THE PLAY OF THE YEAR.**

FUN FACT >>> THE FRONT COVER OF THIS BOOK SHOWS AARON THROWING A FOOTBALL TO HIS WIFE IN THE 300 LEVEL OF THE SUPERDOME AFTER A SCORE. HE MISSED BY JUST FOUR ROWS. THE PERSON WHO CAUGHT IT REFUSED TO GIVE THE BALL TO TISA.

41

INSIDE THE HUDDLE

Our huddles aren't always so serious. Saints lineman Wayne Gandy made me a deal. He'd block if I told him a joke every game. I don't tell a lot of jokes, but we poke fun at each other. I'll say to a lineman, "Suck in that gut." Or I'll ask a receiver, "Why don't you catch the ball with your big nose." It's important to laugh a little, especially while under stress.

> Michael Vick and I on the sidelines after our teams faced off. Michael was injured and didn't play.
> Tisa and I accept the Humanitarian Award from Pat Shannon, a Boys & Girls Club representative.

HUMANITARIAN AND GOOD GUY AWARDS

The National Quarterback Club named Aaron their winner of the 2004 Humanitarian of the Year Award. He was honored for his community work in both the New Orleans and Newport News, Virginia, communities.

The Sportings News named Aaron one of the NFL's "Good Guys," for his role in an annual Internet video chat with second cousin (and Falcons QB) Michael Vick between local children's hospitals, in which terminally ill kids participate. Brooks also started a reading program in his hometown and New Orleans.

> Tisa and I out to dinner with my "little brother" Jaret, who I met through the Waldo Burton Boys Home and Big Brother-Little Brother program.

> My framed high school jersey.
> Speaking to kids at the Read To Pass kickoff event in New Orleans.

In each of the three seasons after our playoff win, we needed just one more victory during the season to reach the post-season. I believe with the right chemistry and proper effort and focus, the Saints will rise above their past and turn into winners.

Now that I've shown what I can do and put my name in a few record books, I don't worry about comparing myself to others or worry about recognition anymore. Maybe I've had a chip on my shoulder. For those who doubted me or who say, "He's a good quarterback, but …" I just point to the numbers and let them speak for themselves.

One of my most cherished honors brought me back to Newport News in June of 2004. Heritage High School school officials placed me in their Hall of Fame and retired my football and basketball jerseys.

It's every kid's dream to have his or her jersey retired at their high school. My school was closed down, but Heritage thought enough about Ferguson to continue its legacy. It's very special to be acknowledged in this way.

I JUST TRY AND LIVE A GOOD LIFE AND HONOR MY WIFE, PARENTS, AND FAMILY, DO MY JOB TO THE BEST OF MY ABILITIES, AND GIVE BACK TO MY COMMUNITY WHEN I CAN.

FUN FACT >>> TISA'S FATHER USED TO ENCOURAGE AARON TO READ A NON-SPORTS SECTION FROM THE NEWSPAPER WHILE HE VISITED SO THEY COULD TALK ABOUT SOMETHING OTHER THAN SPORTS.

If you have a desire to rise above your situation, then make a promise to yourself and make a plan, with the help of mentors you trust. Then follow through with focused energy and stick to it.

Stay out of trouble and don't look for short-cuts. Be willing to do the necessary work. Don't try to be someone you're not. Be proud of who you are.

When times are tough, keep smiling with a positive attitude. When you get knocked down, get back up!

Do what's right and God will take care of you. That's all I try to do.

Most importantly, have faith that you will rise above.

Total Passing Yards, Career		TDs, Career	
Archie Manning	21734	Archie Manning	115
Bobby Herbert	14630	**Aaron Brooks**	**86**
Aaron Brooks	**12464**	Bobby Herbert	85
Jim Everett	10622	Jim Everett	60

Total Passing Yards, Season		TDs, Season	
Jim Everett	3970	**Aaron Brooks**	**27**
Jim Everett	3855	**Aaron Brooks**	**26**
Aaron Brooks	**3832**	Jim Everett	26

Total Passing Yards, Game		TDs, Game	
Aaron Brooks	**441**	Bobby Herbert	6
Archie Manning	377	Jim Everett	6
Jim Everett	376	Billy Kilmer	6
Jim Everett	370		

QB Rating, Career		QB's 250-Yard Games	
Aaron Brooks	**82.1**	**Aaron Brooks**	**21**
Jim Everett	81.1	Archie Manning	20
Bobby Herbert	79.1	Jim Everett	18
		Bobby Herbert	18

QB Rating, Season	
Aaron Brooks	**88.8**
Jim Everett	87.0
Aaron Brooks	**85.7**

* Through the 2003 season

AARON BROOKS STATS
UNIVERSITY OF VIRGINIA

Year	G	Att	Comp	Int	Yards	Pct.	YPG	TD	Long
1994	0	0	0	0	0	0	0	0	0
1995	1	2	0	1	0	0	0	0	0
1996	11	89	37	7	517	41.6	47.0	1	42
1997	11	270	164	7	2,282	60.7	207.4	20	71
1998	11	290	156	9	2,319	53.8	210.8	12	73
Total	34	651	357	24	5,118	54.8	150.5	33	73

AARON BROOKS PRO STATS

Year	Team	G	GS	Att	Comp	Pct	Yards	YPA	Lg	TD	Int	Tkld	20+	40+	Rate
1999	Green Bay	0	0	0	0	—	0	—	0	0	0	0	0	0	—
2000	New Orleans	8	5	194	113	58.2	1514	7.80	53	9	6	15/94	20	4	85.7
2001	New Orleans	16	16	558	312	55.9	3832	6.87	63	26	22	50/330	55	13	76.4
2002	New Orleans	16	16	528	283	53.6	3572	6.77	64	27	15	36/236	47	12	80.1
2003	New Orleans	16	16	518	306	59.1	3546	6.85	76	24	8	34/195	36	7	88.8
Total		56	53	1798	1014	56.4	12464	6.93	76	86	51	135/855	158	36	82.1

> Young players, attending one of the football camps I've sponsored, listen to my instructions.

> A happy camper shows off my old high school colors.

> Kids listen to me and Ruby Bridges talk about the importance of reading at one of my library visits in New Orleans.

THE AARON BROOKS FAMILY FOUNDATION

Dedicated to improve the lives of youth by supporting them in educational and mentorship programs to enhance their ability to become responsible and productive adults.

Initiatives

READ TO PASS PROGRAM

When I was young, I didn't have the patience to sit down and read for pleasure. In middle school, my science teacher created a reading period for us. That helped me out a lot.

Mom always stressed the importance of reading, as she's an avid reader. I became interested in novels during college. To rise above in almost any profession, reading is a key skill. Reading can take you places you've never been before.

Tisa, whose mom is an educator, and I learned that one reason many disadvantaged children fall behind academically is because they don't read during the summer. The "summer loss" of reading takes its toll year after year and can add up to an 80 percent difference by middle school.

So we decided to start "Read To Pass" in 2003. The program teams with city libraries in New Orleans and Newport News to generate interest in summer reading. It also shows families the free resources available at local libraries.

Read To Pass rewards kids for reading eight books or 800 pages during the summer. I visit local libraries to draw kids and families to see what their library can offer. I have visited about a dozen libraries in two years. I read from books, share stories about my life, and sign autographs. We ask kids to sign a pledge that acknowledges the importance of being a life-long reader and to sign up for the Read To Pass summer program. The first summer of Read To Pass, more than 10,000 kids joined the program and read about 80,000 books.

WALDO BURTON BOYS HOME

Shortly after I joined the Saints, I heard about the Waldo Burton Boys Home in New Orleans. It's the oldest boys home in the South, first opening its doors 1824. I learned how the facility provides care, support, guidance, and a safe living environment for young boys. Waldo Burton Boys Home is a beneficiary of our foundation.

Future initiatives

THE AARON BROOKS FAMILY FOUNDATION OUTREACH LIBRARY PROGRAM

This program will develop outreach libraries to serve children who do not have access to libraries.

To volunteer, sponsor, or donate to the Aaron Brooks Family Foundation, contact us at:
3501 N. Causeway Blvd., Suite 321, Metairie, LA, 70002.

Index

Websites

Aaron Brooks official website	www.bigbrooks.com
Green Bay Packers	www.packers.com
Official NFL site for kids	http://www.playfootball.com
National Football League	www.nfl.com
New Orleans Saints	www.neworleanssaints.com
Reading Is Fundamental (RIF)	www.rif.org
University of Virginia	www.virginia.edu